Isle of Skye in the Apple Pie

By

Carolyn Davison

Copyright © Carolyn Davison 2018

The right of Carolyn Davison to be identified as the author of this work has been asserted by her in accordance with the Copyright, Designs and Patents Act, 1988

All rights reserved. This book is sold subject to the condition that it shall not, by way of trade or otherwise, be lent, re-sold, hired out or otherwise circulated in any form of binding or cover other than that in which it is published.
No part of this book may be reproduced, whether by photocopy or by other means nor must any of the content be displayed on a website without prior permission from the author

ISBN: 978-0-9561573-4-8

Dedicated to everybody who is slightly 'off-the-wall'!

A massive thank you to Tim for doing a wonderful editing job for me!

CONTENTS:

Mid Life Cruising

Crime and Education in the Wind?

The World Wide Web of Life

A Season to be Happy and Jolly

Musical Weight Loss

Made in Britain

Batty Books

MID LIFE CRUISING

HORMONES

Hormones are wonderful, hormones are swell,
'Cos they can make yer happy and miserable as well!
And when yer on yer period, yer men can always tell
When yer hormones are whizzing round ya body!

Chorus:
If it wasnae for our hormones what would we be?
We'd be blobs of jelly, with no personality,
'Cos we wouldn't have the moods that swing,
Nor be grumpy
If we didnae have the hormones in our bodies!

And when we're on our monthlies, we wanna scream and shout!
We lock ourselves in our rooms and keep our partners out!
And when they yell "You all right, love?" we wanna give 'em a clout!
That's when they realise we have some hormones!

Chorus:
If it wasnae for our hormones what would we be?
We'd be blobs of jelly, with no personality,
'Cos we wouldn't have the moods that swing,
Nor be grumpy
If we didnae have the hormones in our bodies!

Now when we get pregnant, our hormones go just wild,
We want to eat everything, for the good of the child!
After birth, with sleepless nights, it's easy to get riled,
Because of the extra hormones in our bodies!

Chorus:
If it wasnae for our hormones what would we be?
We'd be blobs of jelly, with no personality,
'Cos we wouldn't have the moods that swing,
Nor be grumpy
If we didnae have the hormones in our bodies!

When we're young we have monthlies, then there's the menopause:
Hot flushes and weight gain; water retention, of course!
Then when we're low, we want to eat perhaps a cow or horse!
That's what we get for having flippin' hormones!

Chorus:
If it wasnae for our hormones what would we be?
We'd be blobs of jelly, with no personality,
'Cos we wouldn't have the moods that swing,
Nor be grumpy
If we didnae have the hormones in our bodies!

PMS BLUES

My stomach has started bloating,
I don't know what to do!
Do I run around screaming –
Creating a hullabaloo?
Or do I sit down quietly,
And listen to sweet sounds?
I hope at my next weigh-in
I haven't gained some pounds!

Oh no! I feel crotchety –
I need some chocolate NOW!
And if I don't get any,
I'll be a grumpy cow!
So watch out all you husbands,
Partners, boyfriends too
If you say anything rotten –
We'll have to scream at you!

Hormones are so wonderful!
You can do as you please!
For one week in the month
Your guys beg on their knees!
"Oh yes, my darling, you can buy
That expensive strapless dress!"
Your guy will do most anything
When under sweet duress!

So come on girls, be strong and brave!
Don't you ever cower!
PMS is something which
Gives a girl her power!

THE SHOPPING TRIP

Dashing through the store,
Wild kids in tow!
Johnny wants some sweets!
Mommy tells him "NO!"
So he throws a strop –
Lying on the floor!
Mommy goes into meltdown mode
And cannot take no more!

Ring those bells,
Ring those bells,
Mommy needs to pay,
But her card has been declined –
It really ain't her day!

Ring those bells,
Ring those bells,
Bertha needs the loo!
Freddy trips and bangs his head,
Mommy don't know what to do!

She fumbles in her bag,
Looking for some cash!
All that she can find
Is lots of kiddy trash!
Tissues full of snot,
Sweety wrappers too!
Mommy's feeling so harassed,
The air is turning blue!

Ring those bells,
Ring those bells,
Mommy's lost the plot!
Other people in the queue
Are getting rather hot!

Ring those bells,
Ring those bells,
Mom's about to flip!
If the kids won't quieten up –
Each one will get a clip!

She finds a 20 note
Folded in her purse,
Hands it to the girl
But things are getting worse!
Bobby punches Jim,
Jane begins to shout!
Mommy begins to yell and scream
"Why did I bring you out?"

Ring those bells,
Ring those bells,
Mommy needs to pack!
Amy's pulling Danny's hair
And Ben is kicking Zack!

Ring those bells,
Ring those bells,
Mommy needs a shrink!
Baby Chaz has pooped his pants!
Now the store will really stink!

Mommy grabs her bags,
Dashes for the door,
Lots of kids behind,
Skidding on the floor!
Counting all of them
And feeling rather blue,
She begins to realise
That Bertha's in the loo!

Ring those bells,
Ring those bells,
Kiddy left behind!
Mommy thinks she needs a break
Before losing her mind!

Ring those bells,
Ring those bells,
Soon they all get home!
Mommy goes and hides away
'Cos her poor nerves are blown!

THE SHOPPING BAG

We are told to avoid all plastic bags:
They're not good for planet Earth,
So I bought myself a stringy bag;
Skipped to the shop with mirth.

It started off so tiny,
I wondered if it would cope
With all the things I had to buy,
From tins to bars of soap!

Trolley loaded to the brim!
I was as proud as proud can be,
I was helping the environment
With my bag so small and stretchy!

I waited in the checkout line,
Carrier firmly in my hand!
Proud I was of that stringy bag -
I was going to save this land!

The lady behind the checkout desk
Scanned everything in my trolley.
I started to put things in that bag -
I was feeling rather jolly!

The bag began to stretch right out -
It became twice its normal size!
I shoved and squeezed, puffed out my cheeks;
I really was surprised.

The amount of things that bag could hold
Amazed everyone in that store,
Because when I thought it was done
I could squeeze in something more.

The food kept coming down the belt.
My bag was becoming huge,
But still I pushed and shoved things in!
My face was rather rouge.

That stringy bag I thought would break,
But it was strong as steel.
I filled and filled it to the brim
With every kind of meal!

When at last I came to pay,
My look changed from proud, to funny,
Because I'd not brought my leather bag
Which contained all my money.

So with a face as red as fire
I had to unpack that bag.
The woman behind the checkout desk
Was looking rather mad!

The manager came over to me
And waved his great big hand!
And said in angry, vicious tones
"Do this again and you'll be banned!"

So all forlorn, I left that place!
Stringy bag shrunk to normal size!
Looking back at the superstore
I wiped large tears from my eyes!

The moral of the story is:
You may want to save this land,
But make sure you bring your money with you
To stop you from being banned!

MOLAR

I went into the room and I sat in the chair
Where the dentist said I thought that I had told ya
T-O-L-D told ya!
He walked up to me and said, "Open wide!"
I looked very scared, even more when he cried MOLAR
M-O-L-A Molar mo-mo-mo-mo- molar!

Well I'm not usually one to cry,
But when he brought out his pliers there's a tear in my eye!
Oh my molar, mo-mo-mo-mo- molar!
Well I closed my eyes and clung to his hand
And wouldn't let go, like a rubber band!
Oh my molar, mo-mo-mo-mo- molar, mo-mo-mo-mo- molar

Well he pulled and he pulled with all his might
Under his electric light!
He asked for assistance from the guy next door,
Who said, "It might be better if she lay..."
I'm not usually someone to moan
But when I looked at those pliers, I felt a loss for my molar
mo-mo-mo-mo- molar, mo-mo-mo-mo- molar
Molar mo-mo-mo-mo- molar, mo-mo-mo-mo- molar

I jumped out the chair!
I ran to the door!
I slipped to the floor!
I got up on my knees!
I looked at him, and he at me!

I like my tooth and I want it to stay,
And really I want it to be that way for my molar
mo-mo-mo-mo- molar!
I like my teeth and my teeth like me
It's just the way I really want it to be
for my molar, mo-mo-mo-mo- molar!

Well I had a pain the week before
And I can say it ain't bad anymore.
The dentist smiled and said "You'll be fine;
I missed the molar, took out a canine!"
I looked in the mirror and saw the gap!
Went away, still a happy chap,
For my molar
mo-mo-mo-mo- molar
mo-mo-mo-mo- molar
Molar mo-mo-mo-mo- molar!

SCOOTER AND SHOES BLUES

Sitting on my bum all day
Staring at the 'puter,
When an idea came to me!
Why don't I buy a scooter –

The type you see on all the streets.
The one that children use.
Didn't know how it would work out
While wearing my 3 inch shoes!

I nipped into my local store
And bought one – pink and shiny!
I was hoping no-one laughed at me
Or else I'd become whiney!

I started off wonderfully,
Zipping down the road!
Feeling like a child again,
Free of all workload!

Suddenly I realised
There were no blessèd brakes!
I knew in my heart of hearts
Those shoes I would forsake!

I dug my heels into the ground
And heard a noise I'd hate!
While trying to stop this confounded thing
My shoes caught in a grate!

As fast as I had started,
My scooter, it did stop,
But I kept moving forward
And flew over the top!

My shoes were in an awful mess -
The heels were left behind
In that blasted street grate,
For someone else to find!

The moral of the story is –
Don't wear 3 inch shoes
If you go on a scooter
Because you'll get the blues!

THE BASKET

It sat there in the basket;
I was scared as can be!
Was it my imagination
Or was it watching me?

I stood there for a moment,
Wondering what to do!
What was that in the basket?
Should I call the zoo?

I grabbed the phone and dialled;
I called my lovely mum.
I really needed to find out
From where that thing had come!

"Hello my dear. What do you want?"
She spoke in gentle tones!
"Oh mum!" I cried, "Please come here
To my cosy home!"

She grabbed her coat so quickly,
And rushed out of her door!
She came over to my place,
So she could find out more!

I grabbed her arm so tightly,
With fear upon my face!
I dragged her to the kitchen,
And pointed to that place!

"Mum, what is it?" I cried out loud,
Tears rolling down my cheek!
But mum was curled up laughing
And feeling very weak!

After a while she became composed,
And gave a great big smile!
"Don't worry my daughter," she said to me,
"It's just the ironing pile!"

CRIME AND EDUCATION IN THE WIND?

BAKED BEAN HEIST!

Chorus:

Robin Hood
Robin Hood
Cutting through the van!
Robin Hood
Robin Hood
Nicked a load of cans!
Baked beans are tinned –
Causing lots of wind,
Round the 'hood
Round the 'hood
Round the 'hood

He came upon the lorry
Which was parked near the green!
He thought it would be fun to take some beans!
So he got out his cutters;
Made a hole in the side!
Hoping he would not be seen!

Chorus:

Robin Hood
Robin Hood
Cutting through the van!
Robin Hood
Robin Hood
Nicked a load of cans!
Baked beans are tinned –
Causing lots of wind,
Round the 'hood
Round the 'hood
Round the 'hood

The police became suspicious
When they caught an awful whiff;
They wondered if it was a stink bomb!
They brought along their blood hounds
And chased it to its "sauce"!
Those doggies are never ever wrong!

Chorus:

Robin Hood
Robin Hood
Cutting through the van!
Robin Hood
Robin Hood
Nicked a load of cans!
Baked beans are tinned –
Causing lots of wind,
Round the 'hood
Round the 'hood
Round the 'hood

So now that poor old Robin
Is sitting in his cell,
Dreaming up escape plots and plans!
He's given one big parcel!
Can he believe his luck?
Oh no, they're even more cans!

Chorus:

Robin Hood
Robin Hood
Cutting through the van!
Robin Hood
Robin Hood
Nicked a load of cans!
Baked beans are tinned –
Causing lots of wind,
Round the 'hood
Round the 'hood
Round the 'hood

FLOATING IN A PSYCHEDELIC LAND

Sitting down by the fire,
Smoking pot; getting higher!
Puffing all day -
The old hippy way,
Floating in a psychedelic land!

Sky full of diamonds!
Lucy's tripping with Simon,
Marmalade trees,
Kaleidoscope bees,
Floating in a psychedelic land!

In the meadow we can grow some hash, man,
And hope the cops don't call around!
If they do and find our stash, man,
We will have to run and go to ground.

Running 'round chasing dragons;
Drinking gin by the flagon,
Spaced out tonight,
High as a kite!
Floating in a psychedelic land!

THE NIGHT BEFORE SCHOOL

'Twas the night before school
And lying in bed,
Was poor 'little' Johnny
Living in dread!
He sank under his duvet,
And tried not to cry.
All he could mutter was
"Why me? Oh, why?"

He tossed and he turned,
As he thought about school!
If his peers could see him
They'd say – "You're not cool!
Just stop being a wally
A nerd and a drip!
Tomorrow's the day of the
Annual school trip!"

He turned and he tossed,
And threw back the sheets!
Sweat on his forehead
And sweat on his feet!
He thought of the journey
To Accrington Zoo –
And wondered, just wondered,
What the others would do!

He worried and panicked,
And felt for his life!
Until he was prodded
By his dear wife!
"Now stop being silly,
It won't be a disaster!
You have to remember,
You are the Headmaster!"

THE FLUTE EXAMINER

He sat there in the corner,
Glasses poised upon his nose –
Looking over the top of them,
With a very superior pose!

I raised my flute up to my lips
And gave a mighty blow,
But nothing came out of it,
So I turned a reddish glow!

He raised an eyebrow, very high.
He looked rather not amused!
I tried, again, to get a note,
But I was much bemused!

The silly thing wouldn't make
A beautiful haunting sound,
So I gave it an almighty blow -
My cloth fell to the ground!

I looked back at the man sat there,
Not a smile upon his face!
I thought I'd better play my tune
Before I left that place!

So off I went again to try
To play my pretty tunes!
This time I blew – a note came out -
Not a minute or so too soon!

My tune went loud, then went quiet!
Largo, then Allegro.
I had to play some chromatic scales
And one or two arpeggios!

Up and down my scales I raced –
Like a mighty rushing wind!
My minors didn't sound too good
His look was like I'd sinned!

All through the exam he sat and wrote,
Upon his clean white pad!
I wondered if he ever thought
I was good or bad?

"Thank you, sir!" I said to him,
About to leave the room!
When over his glasses, he looked at me,
And in a mighty voice, did boom!

"But wait; you cannot leave me yet,
For you still have not finished!"
He played some notes and I had to choose:
Dominant or diminished!

Shaking like a leaf, I stood,
By the grand pianoforte!
I felt like I wasn't good,
But very, very naughty!

He played a piece and I had to choose
Whether it was fast or slow,
Or if it went very loud,
Or had a dim-in-u-endo!

I breathed a huge sigh of relief
When he told me it had ended!
I dropped my flute upon his foot!
It's not what I'd intended!

I picked up my flute and hurriedly
Put it in its case!
I threw my music into my bag
And hurried from that place!

Before they posted my results,
A while I had to wait!
But good news when the marks arrived!
I passed with one hundred and eight!

ODE TO STORM DORIS (2017)

When I was just a little breeze,
I asked the rainbow – what will I be?
Will I be fierce? Will I be strong?
Will I knock down some trees?

Chorus:

Que sera, sera,
Whatever will be, will be,
Chaos and strife we'll see
Que sera, sera!

Then I became a little gale,
Whistling through branches, churning up leaves!
Breaking umbrellas, stealing some hats –
Just like a band of thieves!

Chorus:

Que sera, sera…

Now I am quite the massive storm!
People are frightened, scared as can be!
Trees on the highway, snow on the hills
Gigantic waves at sea!

Chorus

Que sera, sera…

THE WORLD WIDE WEB OF LIFE

SOCIAL NETWORKING SONG

Facebook and Tumblr,
Twitter and Bebo,
Webcast and Blogger,
MySpace and Skibo,
Zoopla and Flikr
And many more sites!
I'm on the 'puter
All day and night!

Youtube and WeeWorld,
Wooxie and Xanga.
Social network sites
If you like Manga!
Something Delicious,
Asiaworld too!
Social networking -
Whatever you do

LinkedIn and Goodreads,
Google+, Hotlist,
Face Party, Goodwizz,
Anything I've missed?
Hyves, Ibibo,
Itsmy, Jaiku!
There's social networking
Just for you.

Give me a Hi5!
Keep me a-live!
Friends Reunited too,
Buzznet and Cloob,
Cyworld and Govloop
Then we have Exploroo!

ODE TO FACEBOOK

Did you not see my profile?
I changed the picture last week!
I have two thousand and one friends,
And the information I did tweak!
O saw you not my profile
On your computer screen?
I am the one with glasses
Who sometimes looks so mean!

Though they are nothing to me,
Though I never play them,
I have some applications!
I'll have them 'til I die!

Saw you not my profile?
I'm now a right-wing Jedi!
My photos look so crazy
Because they've all got red eyes!
But saw you not my profile?
Just look at it again -
I'm the one with frown lines
Who looks a bit insane!

WHAT SHALL I PUT ON MY FACEBOOK PROFILE?

What shall I put on my Facebook status?
What shall I put on my Facebook status?
What shall I put on my Facebook status?
In the early hours of morning?

Chorus:

Hurrah and up I post it!
Hurrah and up I post it!
Hurrah and up I post it!
In the early hours of morning!

Shall I put something inane?
Shall I put something mundane?
Shall I put "I'm feeling insane"?
In the early hours of morning!

Chorus:

Hurrah and up I post it...

I can't stand my Aunty Netta,
If I post it, I'll feel better!
I may get a nasty letter!
Through the post in the morning!

Chorus:

Hurrah and up I post it…

I shall write – "I hate my job!
And my boss, whose name is Bob!"
I shall say "The temp's a slob!"
In the early hours of morning!

Chorus:

Hurrah and up I post it…

Oh dear, I've got a text
From the boss – he's not impressed!
I'm feeling very stressed –
I have no job in the morning!

Chorus:

Hurrah and up I post it…

X FACTOR BLUES

I'm sitting in the waiting area,
Nerves as strong as steel!
I know that I can win this year -
I have the X Factor for real!

I have my number on my chest;
My spandex suit squeezed on!
And I am ready to go in there
And sing that blessèd song!

I know I am simply the best!
My voice is unique as can be!
I know that I will be signed up
When the judges listen to me!

I get up when my number's called,
I stride right through that door;
I know that when I've finished,
They'll be begging me for more!

I go and stand upon the X,
And give them all my name!
I tell them I am good enough
For glory and for fame!

They ask me who I think I'm like.
I answer, "Just like Elvis!"
I open up my mouth to sing,
And wiggle my enormous pelvis!

A sound comes out - I think it's good!
The judges disagree;
Simon Cowell says I'm naff -
The others don't like me!

I strut up to the desk they're by,
To give a piece of my mind!
I curse and swear and ask them
"How can you be unkind?"

"I've 'ad singing lessons since I were 2,
My mum thinks I am great!
So what do all you judges know?"
I really am irate!

Simon says, "Well look, you see,
Talent you surely lack!
Please choose a different career
And don't ever come back!"

I say, "I'll make a million quid!
I don't need folks like you,
Telling me how to sing!
There's nowt else I wanna do!"

Then pipes up Louis Walsh and says,
"But you're completely duff -
By the time you'd got through half your song,
I'd really had enough!"

Cheryl in her gentle tones,
Tried to make my spirits lift,
And says, "You cannot sing, my dear -
But you must have another gift!"

My heart is broken, my dreams in tatters,
I really wanted that record deal!
I feel right down in those awful dumps -
No-one knows how I feel!

I go out of the audition place,
Knowing I've made a boob!
But you know what, I got internet fame
'Cos my audition's on Youtube!

THE NIGHT BEFORE WORK

'Twas the night before work,
And sat on the chair
Was an employee
Blow-drying her hair.
She had to look good
For the following day,
Standing by the till
Where customers pay.

Suddenly she remembered
She'd forgotten to clean
Two of the fridges
What could this mean?
And then came to mind
The grocery zone!
Oh no, what a pain;
Would the manager moan?

She started to stress
As she blow-dried her hair!
Would her colleagues complain
And say - "That's not fair!
You've left us to tidy,
To clean and to stack.
Just get a grip
Or you'll get the sack!"

Stress building up!
She began to cry
As she thought of the muffins
And sweet apple pie!
The broken wine bottles,
The spilled whipping cream!
She was feeling, oh feeling
That this was extreme!

She thought of the manager -
What would he say
When she went in
The following day?
"Pull yourself together;
Stop being a prat!
You know what to do!"
Would he give her a slap?

As she thought of the next day
She was so full of tension!
Would her contract be ended
Or have an extension?
She was oh so worried
That she wanted to scream,
But suddenly she woke up -
It was only a dream!

THE NIGHT BEFORE AUDIT

'Twas the night before audit
And lying in bed
Was poor frightened Dizzy
Shaking with dread!
What would he ask her?
Would she reply?
Or would she just stand there
And try not to cry?

She tried not to think
Of that awful day,
When the auditors would come
And throw questions
Her way!
She thought of her memory
Which had failed more than once!
Could she get full marks
Or be labelled a dunce?

She quivered and quaked
And tried not to fret
As she thought of tomorrow
Which hadn't come yet!
Would she remember
That something called WEEE
Wasn't a game console
To play, when you're free...?

So as she lay there
Living in dread;
Her brain ticking over
In her warm bed;
Now what's happening tomorrow?
She started to cough;
Oh, what a nutter
It is her day off!

Disclaimer for the following poems: These have not been endorsed by Avon Products Inc.

AVON WORLD

Some buy from me, some just diss me -
I think that's OK!
If I don't give refunds or credit
They will walk away!

They can choose and they can buy
From pages that are bright;
The customer with the cold hard cash
Is nearly always right,

Chorus:
'Cause they are
Buying from the Avon world,
And I am the Avon girl!
You know that they are buying from the Avon world,
And I am the Avon girl!

Some like perfume, some like make-up;
That's all right with me.
Some don't order from my brochure;
I have to let them be!

Some use skincare and some use deo!
I just hope they pay!
Only those who spend their pennies
Make my rainy day,

Chorus:
            'Cause they are
            Buying from the Avon world,
            And I am the Avon girl!
You know that they are buying from the Avon world,
            And I am the Avon girl!

Some sign-up and some say no
When I knock at their doors!
Some just can't stop selling Avon
And want to sell lots more!

People come and people go -
But that's all right, you see
Sales Leadership has made me rich;
I'm always on T.V.

Chorus:
            'Cause we are
            Buying into the Avon world,
            And I am the Avon girl!
You know that we are buying into the Avon world,
            And I am the Avon girl!

DID YOU NOT SEE THE BROCHURE?

Did you not see the brochure?
I posted it through your front door.
I hope you see the offers,
And want to order a lot more!
Oh saw you not my brochure
As it landed on your mat?
Avon sells more than make-up
What do you think of that?

Though not all will look at it!
Some may put it in the bin!
They don't know what they're missing!
The products are so fab!

Did you not see my lipstick?
Its bright and shiny wrapper!
And my trendy handbag,
I'm looking very dapper!
Oh saw you not my blusher
Brushed on my rounded cheeks?
I order all the products
Every 3 weeks!

MY AVON THINGS

Creams in the cupboard,
And gels in the shower!
Avon cosmetics gives
Each girl some power!
Make up in drawers and
Necklace and rings;
These are a few of my Avon things!

PJs in wardrobe,
And soap on the white sink,
Fragrance and powders,
Which give out a nice stink!
Splash on for our blokes;
They smell just like kings!
These are a few of my Avon things!

Lotions for wrinkles,
And shampoo for all hair.
Of course we look great -
People stop and stare!
Toys for our kiddies,
Lots of shining bling!
These are a few of my Avon things!

When the crunch bites,
When the bills sting,
When things are getting bad,
We all take our brochures and put them through doors -
Avon makes us so glad!

DING DONG BELLS – AN AVON CHRISTMAS

Dashing through the snow,
Delivering Avon books.
Sliding as I go,
Over frozen brooks!
Bells on door posts ring,
People turn on lights,
I am burning calories
On this frozen night!

Ding dong bells
Ding dong bells
Avon calling soon
The sky is clear
As clear as day
I can see the moon!

OH

Ding dong bells
Ding dong bells
Avon calling here -
Order all your brilliant gifts –
You want the latest gear!

A day or two ago
I took some brochures out;
Slipped on the black ice
How I did shout!
People opened doors,
And came to have a look,
So I took a great big chance
And gave them all a book

Ding dong bells
Ding dong bells
Avon calling soon
The sky is clear
As clear as day
I can see the moon!

OH

Ding dong bells
Ding dong bells
Avon calling here
Order all your brilliant gifts -
You want the latest gear!

UP ON THE ROOFTOP – AVON STYLE

Up on the roof top reindeer pause,
Out jumps good ol' Santa Claus!
He looks so miffed as miffed can be
Cos everyone's bought Avon from me!

Ho ho ho!
He didn't go,
Ho ho ho
He didn't go,
Up on the rooftop
Click click click.
No more chimney
For good Saint Nick!

First comes the lippy for little Nell!
Good ol' Avon - with its smells!
Put in mascara - Yes that's right,
She'll look good on Christmas night!

Ho ho ho!
He didn't go,
Ho ho ho
He didn't go,
Up on the rooftop
Click click click.
No more chimney
For good Saint Nick!

Next fill the stocking with fragrant treats,
And some blusher for her cheeks!
Here is some jewellery to accessorise!
She will have a wonderful surprise!

Ho ho ho!
He didn't go,
Ho ho ho
He didn't go,
Up on the rooftop
Click click click.
No more chimney
For good Saint Nick!

A SEASON TO BE HAPPY AND JOLLY

SANTA MEETS THE HSE

Up on the rooftop reindeer pause,
Out jumps good ol' Santa Claus.
He's as miffed as miffed can be -
'Cos he's had post from the HSE!

Chorus:

No, no, no, he can't go!
No, no, no, he can't go!
Up on the rooftops
Click, click, click.
No more chimneys
For good Saint Nick!

Dear Santa, no more heights;
You might fall and get a fright!
No heavy lifting, no more fires,
No more skis - only Goodyear Tyres!

Chorus:

No, no, no, he can't go!
No, no, no, he can't go!
Up on the rooftops
Click, click, click.
No more chimneys
For good Saint Nick!

No more flyin' at dead of night -
Unless your sleigh is full of lights.
You can't stereotype the toys -
Guns for girls, and dolls for boys!

Chorus:

No, no, no, he can't go!
No, no, no, he can't go!
Up on the rooftops
Click, click, click.
No more chimneys
For good Saint Nick!

Don't drink sherry left as a surprise,
Or else the police will breathalyse!
No mince pies for you to eat,
Or you will be classed as obese!

No, no, no, he can't go!
No, no, no, he can't go!
Up on the rooftops
Click, click, click.
No more chimneys
For good Saint Nick!

THE NIGHT BEFORE CHRISTMAS (SHOPPING STYLE)

'Twas the night before Christmas
And all through the store
People were demanding
And buying more and more!
They had trolleys laden
With lots of food!
Some were very polite,
But others were rude!

They went down the aisles;
Filled their baskets
With booze!
Some spent like rich people;
I think it a ruse.
They pushed and they shoved
And blocked up the way
To chat to their neighbour
They see every day!

Then they get to the checkout
And stand in the line
Moaning and groaning -
It's taking up time!
They look at their watches
They tut and roll eyes.
Have a go at the cashier -
Well, there's a surprise!

Come on now, people
It's only one day;
It's not like the shop
Is going away!
The staff need a break,
A holiday too!
So stop and think
About others
And not just you.

This is the season
To show some good cheer!
You only have to be happy
One day in a year.
That's one out of 365 days,
It's not going to hurt you
Or make you amazed!

THE DAY AFTER CHRISTMAS

'Twas the day after Christmas
And all through the house
Were plenty of chocolates
Going into my mouth.
Some were all plain,
Others white and milk;
Some were bitter and
Others smooth as silk!

I opened the cupboard
And guess what fell out!
But oodles of biscuits -
Oh, I could shout,
But I kept very calm,
As calm as could be
And opened a box,
And ate twenty-three!

I daren't go on the scales -
I dread what I'd find!
I've probably gained weight -
Oh, what a bind.
Do not worry and
Do not despair;
In a few days' time
We'll be in next year!

CHRISTMAS PUB GRUB

'Twas the night before Christmas
And I sat in the pub,
Waiting and hoping
I was getting nice grub!
I ordered the turkey,
And some Brussels sprouts,
But there came from the kitchen
One terrible shout!

"Everybody run,
Nobody stay –
The Christmas pudding
I tried to flambé!
I didn't use matches,
Nor a chef's small blow torch;
I used something bigger
That could blow up a Porsche!

"I bought it online;
I thought it OK –
Until the pudding
I tried to flambé!
It worked on the dessert,
The plate and the pan –
The cooker exploded
And so did the fan!"

I looked at the chef:
Hair singed on his head;
His big round face
Was glowing bright red!
With my eyes I began to
Look a bit lower;
Believe it or not –
He held a flame thrower!

I've never seen people
Move, Oh so fast!
Everyone got out
Before the big blast!
All that is left
Of that quaint country pub
Are some Brussels sprouts!
So much for my grub!

SANTA'S LITTLE HELPER

'Twas the night before Christmas
And on the mantelpiece shelf,
There sat Santa Claus'
Tiny, green elf!
He gibbered and he giggled –
As daft as could be,
'Cos he'd drunk all the sherry
While under the tree!

He rolled round and round
On that mantelpiece shelf –
That daft little man
Who was Santa's elf!
He slurred all his words,
And swung from the tree!
Played football with the baubles –
Oh, dearie me!

He tore decorations,
And ripped them to shreds,
And made ghoulish noises
While the kids lay in bed!
He opened the fridge
And stomped in the food!
Giggled and gibbered;
Said words which were rude!

He opened the presents
And spread them around!
All of a sudden
He heard a bad sound!
The door to the room
Squeaked on its hinge!
The elf disappeared –
No time to cringe!

There in the middle of
The hullabaloo,
Lay the tired pet dog,
At a loss – what to do?
The elf was long gone
To Santa's fair isle!
The owner just scowled;
Couldn't muster a smile!

Poor little doggie
Was feeling so blue!
He cowered in the corner –
What an awful to-do!
Surrounded by paper,
A wrecked Christmas tree!
A very angry owner,
At half past three!

GNOME IN THE HOME

He sat there in the garden
Miffed as miffed can be,
Getting drenched with the pouring rain
And putting up with doggy wee!

"I've had enough!" he cried out,
"I'm as cold as cold can be!
I'm fed up with pouring rain
And lots of doggy wee!"

So he grabbed his little bundle;
Headed for the home!
That poor dejected ornament,
That little garden gnome!

He saw the lights inside,
And the tiny little elf,
Looking very smug and clean,
Sitting on his shelf!

The gnome was very determined
To knock him down a peg or two,
And maybe, just maybe
Flush him down the loo.

He had dreams of great conquests,
Of starting world war three.
No more rain, no more outdoors,
And no more doggy wee!

He wanted that position,
On the honoured mantel shelf!
He wanted to take the place
Of that smug and smarmy elf!

So he waltzed up to the back door;
Squeezed through the small cat flap.
He was ready and willing
To give that elf a slap.

Striding now with purpose,
Into the lounge he went,
Glaring at that little elf;
War was his intent!

The elf jumped down to greet him,
But got a massive smack,
Which sent him flying in the air,
Then landing on his back.

The elf recovered quickly,
And took a Kung-Fu stance,
He did a few manoeuvres
Kicking Gnomey in the pants!

Not feeling too discouraged,
The gnome rallied around,
And with his big fat belly,
Knocked Elfie to the ground!

The belly was too much
For that skinny smarmy elf,
He groaned and he gibbered
And climbed back to his shelf.

He looked down at Gnomey,
Looking beaten, bashed and bruised!
Sounding very Victorian, shouted out
"I'm not amused!"

Gnomey poked his tongue out,
Blew a raspberry, very loud.
Puffed out his pudgy little chest,
Feeling very proud!

So off went little Gnomey,
Smug as smug can be,
Into the owner's kitchen,
To make a cup of English tea!

MUSICAL WEIGHT LOSS

UP AND DOWN THE SCALES

Up and down the scales I go
Doh, ray, mi, fah, soh:

More like 2,3,4,5,6,
That's more fat upon my hips!

A,B,C,D,E,F,G -
Hear the pretty melody!

One stone, two stone, three stone, four,
Hear those fat cells knock the door!

Major, Minor play those keys
In such beautiful harmonies!

Major disaster, Minor progress -
I think I am going to regress!

Up and down the scales I go,
Doh, ray, mi, fah, soh.

Up and down the scales one goes;
Shame I cannot see my toes!

UP AND DOWN THE SCALES AGAIN

Dough - is full of fat and lard
Ray - a little spark of hope
Me - I can do this with help
Far - long walks; will I cope?

So! I've eaten chips today
Lah a song to follow on
Tea - 2 litres on the way
This then brings us back to dough, dough, dough.

Dough - money to buy food
Tee - exercise on the course
Lah - a cheerful little note
Sow - no seeds of remorse

Far - where we've come so let's not stop
Me - and you let's be strong
Ray - another spark of hope
And
Doh will end this song song song song!

ALPHABET DIETING

Aerobics is something we should all do
Because it's good for our hearts!
Cardiovascular is the buzz word.
Dancing becomes a fine art!

Elegant ladies in skimpy bright tops,
Funky and trendy as well!
Gym's full of women keeping so fit
How they all look really swell!

Imagine a life without any flab,
Jumping and bouncing about -
Kitted in the most fabulous clothes;
Looking forward to all those nights out!

Minis and skimpies, jeans and bikinis,
Nothing would be holding us back!
Ordinary women, becoming princesses;
Perfect, 'cos nothing we lack!

Quests we are on for a body so svelte
Raunchy as raunchy can be!
Sexy and gorgeous, turning all heads
Turning 3-60 degrees!

Under this flab we all wanna be
Vixens wanting to get out!
We should all do our fitness DVDs;
Xcellent then we shall shout!

Y do we falter when it's easy as pie?
Zealous dieters we should be.
So let's get planning our menus and things,
Starting from Ay-Zee!

EARLY MORNING EXERCISE

One morning I got up
To swim at half past 3.
No one was out at that time -
Only little me!

I wrapped up warm for winter,
And went out in the cold;
It burns even more calories -
Or so I have been told.

Briskly I walked from my house,
Arms swinging by my side.
I could not be more smug at all
Even if I tried.

I was going to be the first there;
I would be swimming alone,
And by the time the pool was full
I would be long since gone!

That morning I arrived at 4
And peered through the glass.
No one around, it was good;
I really must be fast.

I sneaked round to the building side
And climbed into the shaft!
I squeezed and squeezed along inside
Feeling very daft.

I thought that I could do it;
I didn't think I'd get stuck.
That's exactly what had happened -
I felt a silly schmuck.

I cried and screamed my lungs out
But no one was in work;
Still I wriggled and I squirmed
And felt a total jerk.

"Help!" I cried, loud as I could,
But it was to no avail.
My idea of morning fitness
Was one big massive FAIL!

I really should have waited
Until the opening time.
'Cos I had to wait in there,
And be caught for my crime.

It must have been at half six
I heard a car pull up.
I felt like a silly wally
'Cos I was very stuck.

Again I screamed and cried for help;
This time I heard a voice.
"Who's in there? Give me your name!"
I had to - there was no choice.

Eventually they got me out;
My face was red as red.
The police, they didn't charge me;
Gave me a stern warning instead.

The news made the paper,
The TV headlines too;
I also have a million fans,
On the site they call YouTube.

GOOD KING WENCESLAS BUYS PIZZA

Good King Wenceslas went out;
Bought pizza for Stephen:
He ordered a big round one -
Deep pan, crisp and even.
Melted was the cheese on it;
Stringy Mozarella!
Stephen ate the whole lot up!
Now he's a happy fella!

EXERCISE A-B-C

A for Aerobics it gets the heart pumping
B for Bungee come on let's get jumping
C for Cardio - we must keep it strong
D for Drumming and singing a song
E for Exercise it keeps us quite trim
F for Foxtrot - let's dance 'til we're slim
G for Golf - let's stay under par
H for Hockey - don't hit it too far
I for Interesting - exercise must be
J for Jumping, but not out of a tree
K for Kite-flying high up in the sky
L for Lunging - it's good for the thighs
M for Marathon - don't forget to train
N for Netball, but not in the rain
O for Octopushy in your local pool
P for Polo - riding horses, how cool!
Q for Queen of the disco you are
R for Rumba - Oh what a star!
S for Salsacise - with a Latino theme
T for Tango - with a hunk, what a dream!
U for Undoing those couch potato habits
V for Volleyball - jump up like some rabbits
W for Watersports - skiing and diving
X for Xtreme sports - how are you surviving?
Y for Yachting - sailing over the waves
Z for Zumba - the latest exercise craze

BLAME IT ON THE CHOCOLATE

My baby's always eatin' and it wouldn't be a bad thing
But I don't get no chocolate; that's no lie!
We spent the night in Reno eatin Jalapeños.
From that night I kissed my waistline goodbye!

Chorus:
Don't blame it on the salad,
Don't blame it on the spinach,
Don't blame it on tomatoes,
Blame it on the chocolate!

That nasty chocolate bugs me, but somehow it deceived me!
Spellbound, I have to buy more from the shop -
It's changed my life completely, now my clothes don't fit me
And my shoes have gone up another size

Chorus:
Don't blame it on the salad,
Don't blame it on the spinach,
Don't blame it on the tomatoes,
Blame it on the chocolate!

I just can't, I just can't
I just can't control my mouth!
I just can't, I just can't
I just can't control my mouth!

This magic food just grooves me; the fish and chips just fools me!
The devilled chicken's got to be eaten tonight!
I'm full of junk and calories; I got heartburn inside me,
Chocolate's even better in France.

Chorus:
Don't blame it on the salad,
Don't blame it on the spinach,
Don't blame it on the tomatoes,
Blame it on the chocolate!

THE NIGHT BEFORE D-DAY (DIET-DAY)

'Twas the night before D-Day
And all through the house
I was munching on food
Like a wee hungry mouse.
Packets of crisps
And biscuits galore,
Toast with much butter -
I just wanted more.

I went to the cupboard
And ate all the sweets -
My jaw getting exercise,
But not my feet.
I must get rid
Of this offending food.
For it to stay there
Would be highly rude.

What else can I eat
So my cupboards are bare?
For tomorrow I start
My diet with flair.
I shovel in the food,
I empty the fridge,
I eat oodles of crisps -
Some smooth and some ridged.

But it must get done.
D-Day starts soon;
Weigh in the morning,
Not afternoon.
I flumped into bed!
Did I hear it creak?
I hope my resolve
Doesn't go weak.

D-Day has arrived;
On the scales I stand!
Oh dear - this weight
Wasn't so planned.
I gained half a stone
From my binge yesterday!
It was my own fault -
What can I say?

LUCY IN THE LYCRA AND SKIMPY THONGS

Picture yourself in some size 10 pyjamas!
Little black dress with backless surprise.
Somebody whistles, you turn around slowly,
Winking your beautiful eyes!

Elastic waist trousers no more to be seen
Tight round your lardy, fat bum!
Look for the girl with the enormous thighs
And she's gone.

Chorus:
*Lucy in the lycra and skimpy thongs
Lucy in the lycra and skimpy thongs
Lucy in the lycra and skimpy thongs*

Ah!

Follow you down to the shops in the centre;
Make sure you're not eating those high calorie pies.
Men in the workplace look at your figure
Not turning away their big eyes.

Never to wear that huge tent-like garment,
Which hid all your flab on your tum.
Climb up the stairs with no wobble or jiggle;
The fat is all gone.

Chorus
Lucy in the lycra and skimpy thongs...

ODE TO DIETING

Once I went to a party,
My plate ladened with food!
Well I didn't really want
To appear awfully rude!

So on went the sausage rolls,
Those little vol au vents!
And I've got to admit it –
Anything I would want!

The pizzas looked so scrummy,
And the sarnies were a treat!
The quiche looked rather special,
And so did the sweet!

There were cheesecakes and gateaux,
Things oozing with cream!
Everything looked delicious –
I felt like I could scream!

Who cares? I spooned it in
To my over-sized bowl!
Everything in large quantities!
Some things were whole!

Oh well there's always tomorrow
To start on my slimming quest!
I promise that tomorrow
I will do my uttermost best!

The only problem is, you see,
Tomorrow never comes!
So if I'm not careful,
I'll still be eating buns!

Just pretend that somebody
Is paying you loads of dosh,
If you lose all your excess weight,
And don't eat too much nosh!

Always think about being svelte,
Tiny and size eight.
You could always go and buy
A tincy wincy plate!

Do not despair dear dieter,
We all have ups and downs!
So if you have a slip-up,
Don't wear those awful frowns!

Brush it off and start again.
Turn over a new page!
Don't be angry with yourself!
Don't fly into a rage!

DON'T CRY FOR ME HEALTHY SALAD

It won't be easy; you'll think it strange,
When I try to explain how I feel –
That I still need the cake, after all I have lost!
I just need chocolate!
All I can feel is that I am so blue!
My hormones are giving me gip!
I understand and hope you do too!

I had to let it happen; I had to eat!
Couldn't stay all my life without junk!
Looking into the cupboard and into the fridge –
I need ice cream,
Running around trying all of the brands,
But nothing impressed me at all!
Not even the one with choc chips!

Chorus

Don't cry for me healthy salad!
The truth is I'll go and diet!
And through my bad days,
I'll always find ways
To lose all the flab
And not look too bad!

And as for fig rolls and as for chips,
I never meant to buy them in –
Though it seemed to the world they were all I desired,
I preferred pizza!
The cheese that's on top made me feel oh so good
And the base was so crispy to chew!
I understand and hope you do too!

Chorus:
Don't cry for me healthy salad!
The truth is I'll go and diet!
And through my bad days,
I'll always find ways
To lose all the flab
And not look too bad!

Have I eaten too much?
There is nothing more I can think of to eat today,
But all you have to do is look at me
To know that I need to lose weight too!

Chorus:
Don't cry for me healthy salad!
The truth is I'll go and diet!
And through my bad days,
I'll always find ways
To lose all the flab
And not look too bad!

I CAN SEE CLEARLY NOW

I can see clearly now my chest has gone;
I can see all obstacles in my way!
Gone are the tractor tyres from 'round my waist!
It's gonna be a great, great dieting day!

I think I can make it now the flab has gone!
I can see all parts of me melt away!
Here is the weight loss I've been praying for!
It's gonna be a great, great dieting day!

Look all around; my BMI is normal now!
Look ahead; I can see what's in front!

I can see clearly now my stomach's gone,
I can see all shoes that are on my feet!
Gone are the size 20 clothes now!
It's gonna be a great, great dieting week!

WHERE HAVE ALL THE FAT CELLS GONE?

Where have all the fat cells gone?
Long time burnt off!
Where have all the fat cells gone?
Long time ago!
Where have all the fat cells gone?
They've been jogged off, ev'ry one!
Oh, I feel slimmer now!
Oh, I feel slimmer now!

Where have all the calories gone?
Long time disappeared!
Where have all the calories gone?
Long time ago!
Where have all the calories gone?
In the gym and on the bikes!
Oh, I feel slimmer now!
Oh, I feel slimmer now!

Where have all the biscuits gone?
Long time thrown away!
Where have all the biscuits gone?
Long time ago!
Where have all the biscuits gone?
In a landfill, ev'ry one!
Oh, I feel slimmer now!
Oh, I feel slimmer now!

BISCUITS IN THE CUPBOARD

Midnight!
What's that sound from the cupboard?
Is it the chocolate digestives
All feeling alone?
In the dim light
They look so scrummy and yummy to me,
And my stomach begins to moan!

Biscuits,
All alone in the cupboard –
They would love some company
In my rumbling tummy!
They could join the crisps and nuts I ate earlier on!
Couldn't help it – they were yummy!

Every packet seems to me
To cry out a warning!
My stomach grumbles,
Then it starts to rumble –
But soon it will be morning!

Daylight!
Should I wait for the sunrise?
Should I really have breakfast?
Oh, I mustn't give in!
If I eat them
I'll feel like I've just given up –
I will throw them in the bin!

ODE TO CRISPS

'Twas the night before weigh-in
And sat on the shelf
Was a packet of crisps,
All by itself!
The flavour was cheddar
And onion too!
I felt like I wanted them,
But what should I do?

I got out of bed,
And crept down the stairs,
Hoping, just hoping,
The pack was still there!
I opened the door,
And peeked inside –
There on the shelf
It sat with such pride!

The shiny black packet
With writing so bold,
Was a brilliant sight –
Wondrous to behold!
My hand snuck in silently
To reach for the pack!
I really, just really
Wanted a snack!

With stealth and precision
I opened the bag,
And took a deep sniff –
Oh, what a drag!
I felt really guilty;
My conscience kicked in.
Should I decide to throw
Them in the bin?

Oh, what a dilemma!
What should I do?
I fancied a snack
At a quarter past two!
I think I should trust
My instinct again,
And throw them away,
And never complain!

So I opened the lid,
And threw them right in
To join the biscuits
At the bottom of the bin!
Then upstairs I went,
Feeling so smug –
Got under my duvet
Feeling very snug!

MADE IN BRITAIN

QUINTESSENTIALLY BRITISH

How do you know if it's gonna snow?
Visit the BBC weather page!
They may be right or they may be wrong -
Please don't get into a fiery rage.
Promised sun, but we get rain!
Wind? Oh no, a hurricane!
Hail, fog and mist, snow, icy roads too.
Winter, spring, seems like May!
4 seasons in one day!
We love our British weather!

What do we do when someone jumps the queue
In the Tesco Extra basket lane?
Do we keep quiet or do we start a riot
In the Tesco Extra basket lane?
On a bus or on a train,
Ferry, coach or aeroplane!
Supermarkets too, 'cos that's what we do -
We stand in a line, feeling smug and fine,
It's in our British chromosomes!

What do we eat when we want a treat?
An ice cream in a 'cardboard' cone.
We like high tea – 'cos it's so fancy:
Jam and cream on a fruit scone.
Fish and chips by raging sea,
Vindaloo? or kedgeree?
Horseradish sauce, with beef of course!
Wimbledon: such a dream -
Strawberries and cream!
Delightful British cooking!

What do we watch on the old TV box
On a Saturday afternoon?
We like our sports, all kinds and sorts
On a Saturday afternoon.
Rugby, football, golf and darts,
Wrestling and martial arts.
We like our pool and play by the rules,
But if someone takes our wicket,
It just ain't cricket!
Our Great British sporting times!

Scots and Irish, they are Gaels;
Welsh, of course they're from Wales.
English from England, Manx - Isle of Man!
Many cities, many towns!
The Queen wears the crown!
We're quintessentially British!

WE ARE THE WELSH

We are not Irish, we are not Scots,
We are not English, definitely not!
We are the Welsh, an ancient race.
With songs and poetry our land is graced.

Mines and steel, mountains and streams,
Eisteddfods, Welsh Cakes, Rugby teams,
Male voice choirs, hills and vales!
We are the Cymry - those from Wales!

Long place names, Llanfair PG
Lots of L's for you to see.
Abers, Llans are very nice,
Only there to confuse the Saes!

Proud and red, our dragon stands -
The most unique of all the lands.
Mae hen wlad fy nhadau, an anthem tells.
Dwynwen, Maelon and mystic wells.

Twm Siôn Cati; Llewelyn's hound;
The Afanc - creature never found.
Myths and tales, from times long past,
The wizard Merlin, a spell to cast.

We are the Welsh, from the Land of Song,
Tom Jones, Bonnie Tyler, their voices strong.
Charlotte Church, Shirley Bassey too
Shakin' Stephens - "Because I love you!"

DON'T WANNA ZERO

Where have all the good tunes gone and where are all the words?
Some are good and some are fine, but mostly they're absurd!
Isn't there a good tune, to play on my guitar?
In this Euro competition, I wanna get real far!

Chorus:
Don't wanna zero, I'm not wanting a zero at the end of the night.
I've gotta be good and I've gotta sing well;
I hope everyone thinks I'm alright!
Don't wanna zero, I'm not wanting a zero in the morning light!
I've gotta be sure and I've gotta be clear,
And I've gotta be good on the mic, on the mic!

Somewhere in the Baltic, and somewhere in the Med
There are people who are judges -
They think I'm off my head!

Singing in the desert, in the Middle Eastern heat,
Everyone always wonders how Israel can compete!

Chorus:
Don't wanna zero, I'm not wanting a zero at the end of the night.
I've gotta be good and I've gotta sing well;
I hope everyone thinks I'm alright!
Don't wanna zero, I'm not wanting a zero in the morning light!
I've gotta be sure and I've gotta be clear,
And I've gotta be good on the mic!

Don't wanna zero, I'm not wanting a zero at the end of the night!

Up in the Urals, there's a person called Vlad,
He wants to come up against me!
I would hope that there's someone somewhere watching me.

Through the Swedes, and the Greeks and the Danes and the French and the Fins,
Tonight's gonna be the night; I know I can win!

Chorus:
Don't wanna zero, I'm not wanting a zero at the end of the night.
I've gotta be good and I've gotta sing well;
I hope everyone thinks I'm alright!
Don't wanna zero, I'm not wanting a zero in the morning light!
I've gotta be sure and I've gotta be clear,
And I've gotta be good on the mic!

Don't wanna zero, I'm not wanting a zero at the end of the night...

I WILL DELIVER

I'm your local restaurant man, I come from Bangalore.
You spend your cash, and in a flash, I'm knocking at your door.
You may order poppadoms and naan bread with your curry.
To get it out so that it's hot, I must be in a hurry.

Chorus:
I will deliver your curry and your rice.
Everything is homemade, so it will be nice.

I'm the local Indian man, I cook with such a passion.
The pan I use, down to my shoes, is the latest fashion.
So what's the point of Vindaloo, when you have no taste buds left?
Your mouth is numb, can't feel your tongue; you start to feel bereft.

Chorus:
I will deliver your curry and your rice.
Everything is homemade, so it will be nice.

Even though you fill your soul,
The curries are still mine -
All mine

We're the Indian restaurant men; we use lots of ghee.
We cook chapatis on the stove and onion bhajis.
We're the Indian restaurant men giving you an invitation
To come and taste the yummy food from our South Asian nation.

Chorus:
*I will deliver your curry and your rice
Everything is homemade, so it will be nice*

Even though you fill your soul
The curries are still mine

BATTY BOOKS

HUNGRY DOGS

By

Nora Bone

BOUNCING BULLETS

By

Ric O'Shea

SITTING ON A FROZEN LAKE

By

I.C. Butt

CHINESE SPY MASTER

By

Aye See Yoo

OWNING TRAINS

By

Ivan Engine

DIGGING GARDENS
By
Ivor Shovel

SHORT SKIRTS
By
Seymour Legg

CAMPANOLOGY
By
Isabelle Ringing

ANCIENT HEADGEAR
By
Vi King-Helmet

ECCENTRIC PEOPLE
By
Izzie Weird

CUTTING GRASS

By

Mo D. Lawn

THEATRE SEATING

By

Rose O'Chairs

SEEKING PEOPLE

By

R. U. There

PRISM PERSPECTIVE

By

Ray O'Light

PERFECT PASTA

By

Al Dente

CHEESY PASTA

By

Mac Aroni

GLORIOUS ENGLAND

By

Al Bion

PSEUDONYMS

By

A. Lias

RUNNING AWAY TO GET MARRIED

By

E. Lope

QUIET MUSIC

By

P. Anno

HOW TO WATER DOWN YOUR MILK

By

Dai Lute

HOW TO DISTRACT A LECTURER

By

Dai Gress

KEEPING THINGS QUIET

By

C. Cret

PERFECT MACAROONS

By

Al Mond

SAILORS' UNIFORMS

By

Belle Bottoms

STOPPING SHIPS

By

Anne Corr

ELECTRONICS FOR DUMMIES

By

Sir Kitt

ALGEBRA FOR BEGINNERS

By

E. Quation

THE MIDDLE OF THE WORLD

By

E. Quator

CLERGY'S PHONE NUMBERS

By

Di Rectory

MAKING EXPLOSIVES

By

Dina Mite

LIGHT PEDALLING

By

Dina Mo

OUTDOOR EATING

By

Al Fresco

UNACCOMPANIED SINGING

By

A. Cappella

PHONES ON THE MOVE

By

Mo Bile

ROLLING YOUR OWN CIGARETTES

By

Nick O'Teen

CARRYING ON IN ADVERSITY

By

Percy Vere

SAT NAV FOR BEGINNERS

By

U. R. Here

BEATING BULLIES

By

Vic Tim Ised

CATCHING THIEVES

By

Adam Then

Saying No in Russia

By

Yuri Fuse

Safe Moles

By

Ben Ine

Safe Steroids

By

Anna Bolic

Looking at Roman Houses

By

A. Trium

Controlling Acne

By

Dianne Nett

CATEGORISING DIFFERENT ITEMS

By

Miss Elaine E. Us

QUICK MUSIC

By

Al Egro

THE DAWN CHORUS

By

Earl E. Riser

GYM WEAR

By

Leo Tard

COLLECTING OLD ITEMS

By

Anne Teak

INDEX OF POEMS

Alphabet Dieting	65
Avon World	41
Baked Bean Heist	21
Basket (The)	18
Biscuits in the Cupboard	80
Blame it on the Chocolate	70
Christmas Pub Grub	55
Day After Christmas (The)	54
Did You Not See the Brochure?	43
Ding Dong Bells - An Avon Christmas	45
Don't Cry for me Healthy Salad	76
Don't Wanna Zero	87
Early Morning Exercise	66
Exercise A-B-C	69
Floating in a Psychedelic Land	24
Flute Examiner (The)	26
Gnome in the Home	59
Good King Wenceslas Buys Pizza	68
Hormones	6
I Can See Clearly Now	78
I Will Deliver	89
Lucy in the Lycra and Skimpy Thongs	73
Molar	14
My Avon Things	44
Night Before Audit (The)	39

Night Before Christmas - Shopping Style (The)	52
Night Before School (The)	25
Night Before Work (The)	37
Ode to Crisps	81
Ode to Dieting	74
Ode to Facebook	32
Ode to Storm Doris (2017)	29
PMS Blues	8
Quintessentially British	84
Santa Meets the HSE	50
Santa's Little Helper	57
Scooter and Shoes Blues	16
Shopping Bag (The)	12
Shopping Trip (The)	9
Social Networking Song	31
The Night Before D-Day (Diet Day)	71
Up and Down the Scales	63
Up and Down the Scales Again	64
Up on the Rooftop - Avon Style	47
We are the Welsh	86
What Shall I Put on My Facebook Profile?	33
Where Have all the Fat Cells Gone	79
X-Factor Blues	35

END NOTE

Thank you for taking the plunge and purchasing this book. I hope you really enjoyed it and had a good laugh.

WHY THE TITLE?

I thought I should explain that I don't want to eat anybody from the Isle of Skye! The title came from realising that the original one I wanted was too plain! I was going to call this book "Pie in the Sky". I decided to look up the cockney rhyming slang for "Pie" and "Sky" and, apparently, "Pie" is "Isle of Skye" and "Sky" is "Apple Pie" – this was a perfect title for somebody who loves word play! So there you have it – I'm not a cannibal!

A VERY, VERY SHORT BIO:

I grew up in Splott, in Cardiff. (Yes, there is a real area of Cardiff called Splott).

I am married to a very patient and amazing guy and we have 2 wonderful grown up sons. We live in South West Wales.

Proceeds from this book will go to the Davison family, "about time the house was done up fund"!

www.ingramcontent.com/pod-product-compliance
Lightning Source LLC
Chambersburg PA
CBHW061453040426
42450CB00007B/1343